Porcupines

by William Hugo

Pioneer Valley Educational Press, Inc.

This is a porcupine.

3

A porcupine is a rodent.

A squirrel is a rodent.

A mouse is a rodent, too.

This porcupine is sleeping in a tree. Some porcupines live in trees.

The porcupine is looking for salt. Porcupines like to eat salt.

Porcupines have long quills.
The quills are sharp.

Here is a baby porcupine.
Look out!
The baby porcupine
has sharp quills, too!

porcupine

quills

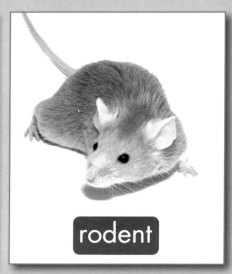

rodent